50 Splenda Recipes

Also by Marlene Koch

Fantastic Food with Splenda: 160 Great Recipes for Meals Low in Sugar, Carbohydrates, Fat, and Calories

Unbelievable Desserts with Splenda: Sweet Treats Low in Sugar, Fat, and Calories

Low-Carb Cocktails : All the Fun and Taste without the Carbs (with Chuck Koch)

50 Splenda Recipes

Favorites from *Fantastic Food with Splenda*, and *Unbelievable Desserts with Splenda*

Marlene Koch

Illustrations by Christopher Dollbaum

M. Evans and Company, Inc.
New York

M. Evans and Company, Inc.
216 East 49th Street
New York, NY 10017

This book offers food that should be enjoyed as part of an overall healthy diet and is not intended as a dietary prescription. Persons with health concerns should seek the advice of a qualified professional, such as a physician or registered dietitian, for a personalized diet plan. Even though the FDA has determined sucralose to be safe for everyone, persons consuming Splenda do so at their own risk. Neither the author nor the publisher is liable for the product and neither is in any way affiliated with the manufacturer, McNeil Specialty Products.

Splenda is a registered trademark of McNeil Specialty Products Company, a Division of McNeil-PPC Inc.

Weight Waters and Winning Points are registered trademarks or Weight Watchers International, Inc. WW point comparisions have been calculated based on published Weight Watchers International, Inc. information and do not imply sponsorship or endorsement of such comparison.

Contents

Cookies and Creamy Favorites

Pies and Crisps

Cakes and Cheesecakes

Quick Smooth Barbecue Sauce

Foreword

About four years ago I discovered Splenda. I was searching for a sugar substitute to include in recipes I was developing for a low-sugar baking class at a culinary academy. The truth is that up until then I had been unable to find an effective no-calorie sweetener for low-sugar baking that would look and taste terrific. Just as I was about to throw in the towel, Splenda came on the market. At first, I thought it was too good to be true—but it wasn't. Not only did Splenda taste like sugar and measure like sugar, it could withstand the heat required for cooking and baking. What's more, it was safe for the entire family (including kids and adults with diabetes). Splenda made it possible to produce great recipes I could be proud of without the calories or added carbs of sugar.

In 2001, my first book, *Unbelievable Desserts with Splenda* was published. I am happy to say this book, with its sweet treats low in calories, sugar, and fat was a great success. Yet people also asked, "Why just dessert?" So three years later, my second book of Splenda recipes, *Fantastic Foods with Splenda*, was published, proving just how versatile Splenda really is. I've used Splenda in recipes ranging from barbecue sauces to salad dressings to meat and fish entrees, and even vegetable side dishes. It is the purpose of this selection of 50 of my favorite Splenda recipes from my two bestselling cookbooks to introduce you to the numerous ways that you can enjoy this wonderful sweetener regardless of taste, occasion, or diet. Try a few of my recipes, and then experiment on your own. I think you will be pleasantly surprised at the quality and taste of the food you prepare using Splenda. Before you begin though, take a few minutes and read the following pages to learn a few tricks of the trade for successfully substituting Splenda for sugar.

When you cook with Splenda, it doesn't matter if you are watching your carbs, simply cutting the sugar, or both, you can enjoy satisfying portions of your favorite sweet foods and desserts again—guilt-free!

What you need to know about Splenda

- Splenda is the brand name for sucralose, the only no-calorie sweetener made from sugar. Sucralose is made through a process that substitutes three chlorine atoms for three hydrogen-oxygen groups on the sugar molecule, producing a substance which the body does not metabolize as sugar but yet retains all of sugar's sweetness.

- Splenda is perfect for all diet plans, including low-carb diets like Atkins' and South Beach, Weight Watchers (the points are included), low calorie plans, and health related diets for diabetes or heart disease.

- Splenda does not affect insulin or blood sugar levels, so it's safe for adults and children with diabetes.

- Splenda tastes like sugar, has no bitter aftertaste, and retains its sweetness even when heated.

- Splenda is safe for people of all ages. Today it's being added to hundreds of products, ranging from foods and beverages to specialty nutritional products and medicines. You won't find any warning labels on Splenda packages.

- Splenda has no calories per teaspoon (as rounded down on the label.) However, low-density carbohydrate is used to "bulk" Splenda Granular for measuring provides 5 calories and 1 gram of carbohydrate per tablespoon. (compared to sugar's 48 calories and 12 grams of carb per tablespoon)

10 Tips for replacing sugar with Splenda in any recipe

While Splenda sweetens like sugar, it's important to remember that it is not sugar. When you cook or bake, sugar does more than just sweeten a recipe; it also contributes to the texture and appearance of many dishes, giving sugary foods their amazing look and consistency. This is why you cannot blindly replace sugar in a recipe with a sugar substitute. The recipes in this book have been created to look and taste as good as their full sugar counterparts—by using a bit of kitchen chemistry. Here's how:

1. Use only Splenda Granular (in the box or bag) because it measures cup for cup like sugar whereas one Splenda packet is equal in sweetness to two teaspoons of sugar

2. Adding small amounts of brown sugar or molasses to a recipe helps to brown foods made with Splenda.

3. A touch of additional leavening, like baking soda or powder gives cakes and muffins the rise they require.

4. Replacing sugar with Splenda may reduce the yield of a recipe. Other ingredients can be adjusted to make up the difference if desired. When baking simply use a smaller pan size if needed.

5. Drop cookies should be flattened with a glass or spatula before baking.

6. Food will bake faster. Check cakes up to 10 minutes sooner, muffins up to 8 minutes sooner, and cookies 3-5 minutes sooner.

7. Syrups and sauces may require additional thickeners. Flour, cornstarch or a low-carb product like Thicken/Thin may be used.

8. Sugar enhances flavor, so you may need to increase amounts of spice (cinnamon, etc) or vanilla to compensate for reducing the in sugar in a recipe.

9. Wrap baked goods tightly in plastic wrap when cooled to keep them fresh. Re-heat in the microwave if desired to bring back that "fresh from the oven" taste.

10. Often just a touch of natural sugar goes a long way in providing the best results in taste and appearance. A few carefully selected teaspoons or tablespoons of sugar add only minimal calories or carbohydrates. Compare that to the usual "cups" of sugar in many recipes (especially baked goods).

About the recipes

All of the recipes in this book were created using Splenda, so be sure to follow them as they are written to insure the best possible taste and appearance. Before you begin to cook, read through this so you understand why certain ingredients must be used:

• Use Splenda Granular (available in the box or bag), not the packets, except where noted.

• Non-fat yogurt can be substituted for low-fat, but do not use "light" or artificially sweetened varieties.

• Choose light whipped topping, not the nonfat version (which contains more sugar and doesn't taste as good).

• When a recipe calls for prune puree, buy baby food prunes or prunes and apples. Or you can make your own by processing 1¼ cups of pitted prunes with 6 tablespoons of hot water until smooth. Sunsweet Lighter Bake can also be used.

• Use only nonstick unflavored vegetable cooking sprays for baking, don't use flavored or olive oil varieties.

- Use real eggs to produce the best flavor and texture. If you must use egg substitutes remember that ? cup is equal to 1 large egg or 2 whites.

- Neufchatel cheese can be substituted for light tub-style cream cheese, but is higher in calories and fat. Full-fat cream cheese significantly increases the calories and fat in a recipe.

- Dutch processed cocoa powder (like Hershey's European) brings a darker, smoother cocoa flavor to low-sugar recipes.

- Use only the type of flour specified in a recipe. Different flours (e.g., cake, whole wheat, or soy) produce different results and may not work in a specific recipe.

- Applesauce should be of the unsweetened variety, only.

- Use your favorite brand of butter or margarine, but never substitute a tub variety unless the recipe specifies it. (Calories and fat were calculated using Land O Lakes 70% vegetable oil/buttermilk blend stick margarine)

Beverages

The amount of sugar it takes to make lemonade is enough to make you pucker. With none of the added sugar, this sweet version is an excellent source of vitamin C.

Ice Cold Lemonade

⅓ cup fresh lemon juice (one large lemon)
or ⅓ cup lemon juice concentrate
2 Tbs Splenda
crushed ice

Pour the lemon juice into a tall (12 ounce) glass. Add the Splenda and stir until dissolved. Add ice to fill the glass. Add water and stir.

One serving

Per serving:

Calories 30
Carbohydrate 8 grams (sugar 0)
Protein 0 grams

Fat 0 grams
Fiber 0 grams
Sodium 0 grams

Diabetic exchange = ½ fruit
WW point comparison = 1 pt

This rendition of the coffeehouse favorite contains only a fraction of the calories. The non-fat half-and-half keeps the mixture silky.

Frosty Mocha

½ cup double-strength coffee or 2 tsp instant coffee dissolved in 4 ounces of warm water (regular or decaffeinated)
¼ cup + I Tbs non-fat half-and-half
3 Tbs Splenda
I tsp unsweetened cocoa powder
I cup crushed ice

Pour the coffee, half-and-half, Splenda, and cocoa powder into a blender. Blend to mix. Add half of the ice and blend briefly (about 15 seconds) until ice is incorporated. Add the rest of the ice and blend once more. Pour into a tall 12-ounce glass.

One serving

Per serving:

Calories 61   Fat 0.5 gram (saturated 0)
Carbohydrate 10 grams   Fiber 0 grams
Protein 2 grams   Sodium 67 milligrams

Diabetic exchange = ½ carbohydrate
WW point comparison= I point

Berries are low in carbs, yet full of phytochemicals (plant compounds that fight against tumors and aging). Any combination of your favorite berries can be substituted.

Berry Blast Smoothie

½   cup 1% (or skim) milk
1   cup plain non-fat yogurt
½   cup blueberries
½   cup frozen strawberries
¼   cup Splenda
1   cup crushed (or cubed) ice

Place milk into a blender. Add remaining ingredients. Pulse. Add ice and bend at high speed until smooth.

Two Servings

Per serving:

Calories 150	Fat 2.5 grams (saturated 1.5)
Carbohydrate 23 grams	Fiber 2 grams
Protein 9 grams	Sodium 145 milligrams

Diabetic exchange = 1 low-fat milk, ½ fruit
WW point comparison = 3 points

This recipe by a Certified Diabetes Educator is a great alternative to high sugar spiced ciders. Keep it warm in a crock-pot for holiday entertaining.

Krista's Spiced Tea

3   cups of boiling water
3   cinnamon stick tea bags
½   cup unsweetened orange juice
1   teaspoon lemon juice
⅓   cup Splenda

Steep tea bags in water for 5 minutes. Remove tea bags and discard. Add orange juice, lemon juice, and Splenda. Stir and serve.

Four servings

Variation: Serve cold with ice.

Per serving:

Calories 15	Fat 0 grams
Carbohydrate 4 grams	Fiber 0 grams
Protein 0 grams	Sodium 0 milligrams

Diabetic exchange = One serving free food
WW point comparison = 0 points

This highly aromatic coffee is perfect to serve with dessert or, with a dollop of whipped topping, as dessert!

Café Orange

6   tablespoons ground coffee (note: Standard coffee scoops often measure 2 tablespoons)

1   small orange

3   tablespoons Splenda Granular (or 4 Splenda packets)

2   teaspoons honey (optional)

4   cups water

Place coffee in filter. Grate peel of orange into grounds.

Measure Splenda and honey into coffee pot. Brew coffee as directed on coffee machine. Add milk or creamer to hot coffee as desired.

Serves Four

Per Serving (with honey)

Calories 20	Fat 0 grams (0 saturated)
Carbohydrate 5 grams	Fiber 0 grams
Protein 0 grams	Sodium 0 milligrams

Diabetic exchange = one serving free food
WW point comparison = 0 points

This rich and filling eggnog is a delicious mini-meal replacement. Try it for breakfast.

Rich, Instant Eggnog for One

1   large egg
1   cup 1% milk
2   tablespoons Splenda Granular
¼   teaspoon nutmeg
1   teaspoon vanilla

Place egg in a large microwavable mug and beat well. Add milk, Splenda, and nutmeg and whisk thoroughly (until egg is completely beaten in).

Heat in the microwave for 1 minute. Stir. Heat for 30 more seconds or until hot and slightly thickened. *Do not boil.* Remove from microwave, stir in vanilla, and enjoy.

Serves One

Per Serving

Calories 180	Fat 7 grams (3 saturated)
Carbohydrate 13 grams	Fiber 0 grams
Protein 15 grams	Sodium 80 milligrams

Diabetic exchange = 1 Low-fat Milk, 1 Medium-fat Meat
WW point comparison = 4 points

Try this satisfying low-calorie beverage to curb your chocolate cravings. It's a delicious alternative to pricy individual packets.

Homemade Hot Chocolate Mix

1	cup nonfat dry milk powder
½	cup nondairy dry creamer
⅔	cup Dutch-process cocoa powder
⅔	cup Splenda Granular

Thoroughly mix all ingredients together. Place into an airtight container. To serve: Stir 3 tablespoons of the dry mix into 6 ounces very hot water.

Serves Fourteen

Per Serving (3 tablespoons)

Calories 45   Fat 1.5 grams (0 saturated)
Carbohydrate 9 grams   Fiber 1 gram
Protein 3 grams   Sodium 30 milligrams

Diabetic exchange = ½ Carbohydrate
WW point comparison = 1 point

Breakfast Treats

Wonderfully moist and light, you'd never guess these are so low in fat and high in fiber. Just be sure to use shredded bran (not bran flakes) for best results.

Banana Bran Muffins

1 cup mashed banana (about 2 medium bananas)

1 cup unsweetened shredded bran cereal (like All-bran)

¼ cup buttermilk

2 large egg whites

2 tablespoons canola oil

2 teaspoons molasses

1 teaspoon vanilla

1 cup all-purpose flour

¼ cup Splenda Granular

1 teaspoon baking soda

1 teaspoon baking powder

½ teaspoon cream of tartar

Preheat oven to 400°F. Spray muffin tin with nonstick baking spray.

In a medium bowl stir together the first 7 ingredients. Set aside for at least 5 minutes to soften bran.

In a large bowl combine flour, Splenda, baking soda, baking powder, and cream of tartar. Stir; make a well and add the liquid mixture, stirring just until blended. Spoon into prepared muffin cups.

Bake for 15 minutes or until center springs back when lightly touched. Cool for 5 minutes before removing to a wire rack.

Serves Twelve

Per Serving

Calories 110   Fat 3 grams (0 saturated)
Carbohydrate 19 grams   Fiber 3 grams
Protein 3 grams   Sodium 220 milligrams

Diabetic exchange = 1 Carbohydrate, ½ Fat
WW point comparison = 2 points

Fresh blueberries give these delectable scones their best appearance; frozen ones will give you "blue" berry scones.

Fresh Blueberry Scones

2	cups all-purpose flour
1/3	cup Splenda Granular
2	teaspoons baking powder
1/2	teaspoon baking soda
1/4	teaspoon salt
1	cup fresh blueberries
1	cup buttermilk
3	tablespoons margarine, melted
1	large egg
1/2	teaspoon almond extract
2	teaspoons granulated sugar

Preheat oven to 425°F. Spray a cookie sheet with nonstick cooking spray.

In a large bowl mix together the flour, Splenda, baking powder, baking soda, and salt. Stir in blueberries; set aside.

In a small bowl whisk together the buttermilk, margarine, egg, and almond extract. Pour wet mixture over dry ingredients and stir just until dry ingredients are moistened (do not overmix).

Drop by heaping spoonfuls (about ¼ cup) onto prepared baking pan, making 13 mounds. Sprinkle scones with granulated sugar. Bake for 12–15 minutes until lightly browned. Transfer to a wire rack to cool slightly before serving.

Serves Thirteen

Per Serving

Calories 115	Fat 3 grams (0 saturated)
Carbohydrate 18 grams	Fiber 1 gram
Protein 3 grams	Sodium 220 milligrams

Diabetic exchange = 1 Carbohydrate, 1 Fat
WW point comparison = 2 points

This holiday favorite can also be made as muffins. Simply spoon batter into 12 greased muffin cups and bake at 375 degrees for 20 minutes.

Pumpkin Pecan Bread

¼   cup canola oil
1   cup pumpkin purée
1   large egg
1   large egg white
½   cup low-fat buttermilk
2   Tbs molasses
1   cup + 2 Tbs Splenda Granular
1¾ cup all-purpose flour
1   tsp baking powder
½   tsp baking soda
1½ tsp cinnamon
½   tsp ginger
¼   tsp cloves
⅓   cup chopped pecans

Preheat oven to 350 F. Coat a 9 × 5-inch loaf pan with nonstick cooking spray.

In a medium bowl, whisk together the oil, pumpkin, whole egg, egg white, buttermilk, molasses, and Splenda. In a large bowl, measure the flour, baking powder, baking soda, spices, and nuts.

Stir and make a well in the center of the dry ingredients. Pour the pumpkin mixture into the well and stir just until all flour is moistened. Do not overmix.

Spoon the batter into the prepared pan and bake for 40 minutes until the crack appears dry and a toothpick placed into the center of the bread comes out clean. Allow the bread to cool in the pan for 10 minutes. Remove the loaf from pan and set back on rack to finish cooling.

Twelve servings

Per serving:

Calories 170	Fat 7 grams (saturated 0.5)
Carbohydrate 22 grams	Fiber 1 gram (sugar 4)
Protein 4 grams	Sodium 170 milligrams

Diabetic exchange = 1½ carbohydrate, 1 fat
WW point comparison = 4 points

This tender and very light-textured cake may very well become your next Christmas classic.

Gingerbread Coffeecake

| 1 | cup all-purpose flour
| ½ | cup Splenda Granular
| ¾ | tsp cinnamon
| ¾ | tsp ginger
| ¼ | tsp allspice
| 4 | Tbs margarine
| ¾ | tsp baking powder
| ½ | tsp baking soda
| ½ | cup low fat buttermilk
| 1 | Tbs + 2 tsp molasses
| 1 | large egg
| 1 | Tbs Splenda Granular
| 1 | tsp cinnamon

Preheat oven to 350 degrees. Spray an 8-inch round cake pan with nonstick cooking spray.

Stir flour and lightly measure 1 cup. Combine flour, ½ cup Splenda, and spices in a large bowl. Cut in the margarine using a pastry blender or fork until the mixture resembles small crumbs. Measure out ⅓ cup and set aside.

To the large bowl of flour, add the baking powder, baking soda, buttermilk, molasses, and egg. Beat with a spoon or on low speed with a mixer until smooth.

Spoon into the prepared pan. Add the tablespoon of Splenda and teaspoon of cinnamon to the reserved crumb mixture. Sprinkle mixture over the top of the cake. Bake for 25 minutes or until the center of the cake springs back when touched lightly.

Eight servings

Per serving

Calories 130	Fat 6 grams (saturated 1.5)
Carbohydrate 17 grams	Fiber 0.5 grams
Protein 3 grams	Sodium 200 milligrams

Diabetic exchange = 1 carbohydrate, 1 fat
WW point comparison = 3 points

This very "quick" cake is made with low-fat baking mix. Just add a good cup of coffee and the morning paper and you're all set!

Quick Cake with Coconut and Almonds

1½ cups reduced fat baking mix (like Reduced Fat Bisquick)

½ cup Splenda Granular

½ tsp baking powder

⅔ cup 1% or skim milk

1 large egg

1 Tbs canola oil

½ tsp vanilla

6 Tbs shredded coconut

2 Tbs Splenda Granular

1 Tbs brown sugar

3 Tbs sliced almonds

1 Tbs melted margarine

Preheat oven to 350 degrees. Spray an 8-inch square baking pan with nonstick cooking spray.

Measure the baking mix, ½ cup Splenda and baking powder into a large mixing bowl. Add the milk, egg, oil, and vanilla. Stir just until smooth. Spoon into prepared pan. Place the coconut, 2 tablespoons Splenda, brown sugar, and almonds in a small bowl. Add the margarine and mix. Sprinkle this mixture over the top of the cake. Bake for 20 minutes or until the center springs back when gently touched.

Nine servings

Per serving:

Calories 160	Fat 7 grams (saturated 2)
Carbohydrate 20 grams	Fiber 1 gram
Protein 3 grams	Sodium 270 milligrams

Diabetic exchange = 1½ carbohydrate, 1 fat
WW point comparison = 3 points

Serve this extraordinary French toast with fresh strawberries and a side of lean ham or sausage to create a beautiful brunch.

Stuffed French Toast

FILLING:

8 ounces light tub-style cream cheese

¼ cup Splenda Granular

2 tablespoons low-sugar strawberry (or other fruit) preserves

EGG MIXTURE:

2 large eggs + 2 egg whites

½ cup nonfat half-and-half

½ cup 1% milk

¼ cup Splenda Granular

2 tablespoons flour

2 teaspoons baking powder

1 teaspoon vanilla

FRENCH TOAST:

16 pieces Italian or French bread (1½ pounds)

1 tablespoon powdered sugar (optional)

Preheat oven to 400°F. Spray baking sheet with cooking spray. Heat griddle or large skillet coated with nonstick cooking spray to medium.

Filling: In a small bowl blend together cream cheese, Splenda, and preserves. Set aside.

Egg Mixture: In a medium bowl whisk together eggs, half-and-half, milk, Splenda, flour, baking powder, and vanilla. Set aside.

Spread 2 tablespoons of cream cheese mixture onto half of bread slices. Top each slice with another piece of bread and press together. Soak each sandwich in egg mixture until saturated but not falling apart. Place sandwich in hot skillet and cook until one side is golden brown. Turn and cook until second side is golden brown. Transfer each piece to baking sheet.

Baked sautéed slices until puffed up and golden brown, about 5 minutes. Dust powdered sugar over tops and serve immediately.

Serves Eight (with powdered sugar)

Per Serving

Calories 270	Fat 7 grams (3 saturated)
Carbohydrate 39 grams	Fiber 2 grams
Protein 12 grams	Sodium 600 milligrams

Diabetic exchange = 2½ Carbohydrate, 1½ Lean Meat
WW point comparison = 5 points

Sweet and creamy, it's almost like a pudding. Try substituting dried cranberries for the raisins and 1 teaspoon of orange zest for the cinnamon.

Baked Oatmeal

OATMEAL:

2	cups old-fashioned oats, uncooked
½	cup Splenda Granular
½	cup raisins*
½	teaspoon cinnamon
½	teaspoon salt
2	cups 1% milk
½	cup nonfat half-and-half
½	cup sugar-free maple syrup
4	large egg whites, lightly beaten
2	tablespoons margarine, melted
2	teaspoons vanilla

TOPPING:

1	tablespoon brown sugar
1	tablespoon Splenda Granular
½	teaspoon cinnamon

Heat oven to 350°F. Spray 1½-quart soufflé dish with cooking spray.

In a large bowl combine the oats, Splenda, raisins, cinnamon, and salt; mix well. In a medium bowl combine milk and remaining liquid ingredients. Add milk mixture to dry ingredients and stir. Pour into baking dish.

Bake for 30 minutes. While baking, prepare topping: Combine brown sugar, Splenda, and cinnamon. Sprinkle on topping and bake for additional 15–20 minutes or until center puffs slightly and is firm to the touch.

Serves Eight

Per Serving

Calories 190

Carbohydrate 24 grams

Protein 8 grams

Fat 4.5 grams (1 saturated)

Fiber 2 grams

Sodium 350 milligrams

Diabetic exchange = 1 Carbohydrate, ½ fruit 1 Fat, ½ Low-fat Milk
WW point comparison = 3 points

*Eliminating the raisins will reduce the carbohydrate by 7 grams per serving.

These low-carb cheesecake cups have as much protein as two eggs—with less fat and calories—Yes!

Breakfast Cheesecake Cups

2   cups 1% cottage cheese
8   ounces tub-style light cream cheese, room temperature
⅔   cup Splenda Granular
½   teaspoon almond extract
½   teaspoon orange zest
2   large eggs
2   large egg whites

Preheat oven to 350°F. Set seven 6-ounce custard cups in a large baking pan (with at least 2-inch sides).

In a food processor, puree cottage cheese until completely smooth. Add cream cheese, Splenda, almond extract, and orange zest; process until smooth. Add eggs and egg whites, one at a time; process to incorporate.

Pour mixture into custard cups. Add hot water to pan until halfway up sides of custard cups. Bake for 25–30 minutes or until set in center. Chill for at least 4 hours. Serve.

Serves Seven (½ cup)

Per Serving

Calories 130   Fat 8 grams (4 saturated)
Carbohydrate 6 grams   Fiber 0 grams
Protein 14 grams   Sodium 380 milligrams

Diabetic exchange = 2 Lean Meat, ½ Carbohydrate
WW point comparison = 3 points

Salads, Vegetables, and Entrees

This version has only half the carbs and calories and one-third the fat of jarred supermarket bean salads.

Classic Three-Bean Salad

1	15-ounce can cut green beans, drained
1	15-ounce can yellow wax beans, drained
1	15-ounce kidney beans, drained and rinsed
1	small green pepper, diced
1	small red pepper, diced
1	small red onion, diced
½	cup red wine vinegar
⅔	cup Splenda Granular
¼	cup tomato juice
3	tablespoons canola oil
¾	teaspoon salt
½	teaspoon pepper

In a large bowl gently mix together beans, green and red peppers, and red onion.

In a small bowl (or jar with lid) whisk (or shake) remaining ingredients.

Pour dressing over bean mixture and toss to coat. Cover and refrigerate at least 6 hours or preferably overnight before serving.

Serves Six (¾ cup)

Per Serving

Calories 165 Fat 6.5 grams (0.5 saturated)
Carbohydrate 22 grams Fiber 7 grams
Protein 6 gram Sodium 360 milligrams

Diabetic exchange = 2 Vegetable, 1 Fat, 1 Very Lean Meat,
                    ½ Carbohydrate
WW point comparison = 2 points

This is at its best when firm and flavorful tomatoes are at the peak of their season. Great for buffets, it can be served hot or cold.

Sweet Italian Tomato Salad

- ⅓ cup white wine (or cider) vinegar
- ⅓ cup Splenda Granular
- 3 tablespoons extra virgin olive oil
- ¾ teaspoon dried basil (or 2 teaspoons fresh, minced)
- ½ teaspoon minced garlic
- ¼ teaspoon salt (or to taste)
- 8 medium tomatoes (about 2½ pounds), quartered and seeded

In a large bowl whisk together all the ingredients except tomatoes. When thoroughly mixed, gently stir in tomatoes. Will keep several days covered in the refrigerator.

Serves Six (¾ cup)

Per Serving

Calories 100 Fat 7 grams (1 saturated)
Carbohydrate 10 grams Fiber 2 grams
Protein 1 gram Sodium 110 milligrams

Diabetic exchange = 2 Vegetables, 1 Fat
WW point comparison = 2 points

The traditional version of this recipe packs in 63 grams of carbohydrate per serving — as much as a piece of fruit pie!

Holiday Cranberry Gelatin Salad

1   12-ounce bag fresh cranberries, washed and picked over
1½ cups Splenda Granular
2   cups boiling water
1   6-ounce box sugar-free cherry gelatin dessert mix
¼   cup granulated sugar
1   cup cold water
1½ cups crushed pineapple (packed in light juice), drained
½   cup finely chopped celery
½   cup chopped nuts

Finely chop cranberries in food processor or by hand and place in medium bowl. Add Splenda and stir. Set aside.

In a large bowl pour boiling water over gelatin and sugar to dissolve. Add cold water. Stir in cranberries, pineapple, celery, and nuts. Pour into 2-quart serving container, mold, or 9 × 13-inch pan and place in refrigerator for several hours or until firm.

Serves Ten (½ cup)

Per Serving

Calories 110   Fat 3.5 grams (2 saturated)
Carbohydrate 17 grams   Fiber 2 grams
Protein 3 grams   Sodium 45 milligrams

Diabetic exchange = 1 Carbohydrate, ½ Fat
WW point comparison = 2 points

A single serving provides a whopping 420 % of the Recommended Daily Allowance for vitamin A.

Silly Carrots

6 cups carrots, peeled and sliced (2 pounds raw carrots)
1 10-ounce can tomato soup (Campbell's Healthy Selections)
⅔ cup Splenda Granular
⅔ cup vinegar
2 tablespoons canola oil
1½ teaspoons prepared mustard
1 medium onion, diced
1 medium green pepper, diced
½ cup celery, chopped
⅛ teaspoon salt

In a medium saucepan cook carrots in boiling water just until tender (about 10 minutes). Drain and set aside.

Combine remaining ingredients in saucepan and cook over medium heat until boiling. Reduce heat and simmer for 10 minutes. Pour over drained carrots. Can be served hot or refrigerated and served cold.

Serves Ten (generous ½ cup)

Per Serving

Calories 90

Carbohydrate 15 grams

Protein 2 grams

Fat 3.5 grams (0 saturated)

Fiber 3 grams

Sodium 180 milligrams

Diabetic exchange = 2½ Vegetable, 1 Fat

WW point comparison = 1 point

These tasty baked "home made" beans can be cooked in the time it takes to prepare a meal.

Stovetop Maple Sugar Baked Beans

1   teaspoon canola oil
1   small onion, finely chopped
½   cup tomato sauce
¼   cup sugar-free maple syrup
¼   cup Splenda Granular
1   tablespoons molasses
2   teaspoons prepared mustard
1   teaspoon vinegar
4–5 drops liquid smoke
2   15-ounce cans pinto beans, drained and rinsed
     (you can vary the beans if you choose)

In a large saucepan heat oil, add onions, and sauté for 3–4 minutes until softened slightly. Add remaining ingredients and stir. Simmer on low for 25–30 minutes.

Serves Six

Per Serving

Calories 145

Carbohydrate 26 grams

Protein 8 grams

Fat 2 grams (2 saturated)

Fiber 5 grams

Sodium 160 milligrams

Diabetic exchange = 1½ Carbohydrates

WW point comparison = 1 point

A terrific lower-carb alternative to sweet potatoes. A nut studded crunchy topping provides the finishing touch.

Butternut Squash Soufflé

SOUFFLÉ:

3	cups cooked mashed butternut squash (about 2 pounds whole)
⅔	cup Splenda Granular
1	large egg
3	egg whites
⅓	cup light sour cream
1	tablespoon margarine, melted
¾	teaspoon cinnamon
½	teaspoon vanilla
1	teaspoon baking powder
¼	teaspoon salt topping

TOPPING:

2	tablespoons flour
3	tablespoons Splenda Granular
3	tablespoons pecans, finely chopped
1	tablespoon margarine, melted
¼	teaspoon cinnamon

Preheat oven to 350.°F Coat a 2-quart casserole or soufflé dish with nonstick cooking spray.

Prepare squash; prick squash with a knife in several

places and place in microwave (whole). Microwave on high for 8–10 minutes. Remove and cut squash in half lengthwise. When cool enough to handle, scoop out seeds. Place halves, cut-side down, in a glass baking dish, add ¼ cup of water, cover tightly with plastic wrap (or lid), and place back in microwave for 10 more minutes or until flesh is very soft. Scoop out flesh into large bowl.

Add remaining soufflé ingredients and beat until well blended. Spoon into baking dish and smooth top.

In a small bowl combine all topping ingredients and mix with fork or fingers until crumbly. Cover top of soufflé with crumb mixture.

Bake for 30–35 minutes until soufflé puffs up in center and top is well browned.

Serves Eight (½ cup)

Per Serving

Calories 120

Fat 5 grams (2 saturated)

Carbohydrate 15 grams

Fiber 3 grams

Protein 4 grams

Sodium 180 milligrams

Diabetic exchange = 1 Carbohydrate, 1 Fat
WW point comparison = 2 points

An easy-to-make favorite that's always a messy hit with kids.

Sloppy Joes

1	pound lean ground sirloin
1	small onion, diced
1	green pepper, diced
4	stalks celery, diced
1	cup water
1	6-ounce can tomato paste
3	tablespoons Splenda Granular
1	tablespoon vinegar
1	tablespoon Worcestershire sauce
½	teaspoon chili powder
½	teaspoon paprika
	Pinch of salt
6	light wheat buns

In a medium skillet, over medium heat, brown beef, onion, green pepper, and celery.

Add remaining ingredients, except buns; mix thoroughly. Reduce heat, and simmer for 20–30 minutes.

Serve scant ½ cup on each bun.

Serves Six

Per Serving

Calories 290	Fat 12 grams (5 saturated)
Carbohydrate 26 grams	Fiber 4 grams
Protein 20 grams	Sodium 500 milligrams

Diabetic exchange = 1½ Carbohydrate, 3 Lean Meat, 1 Fat
WW point comparison = 6 points

Fashioned after the popular "Bourbon Chicken" found at many food courts, this delicious version kicks it up a notch with the addition of real bourbon.

Bourbon Chicken

⅓ cup light soy sauce

⅓ cup Splenda Granular

⅓ cup bourbon whiskey

2 tablespoons dried, minced onion

1 teaspoon molasses

1 teaspoon powdered ginger

½ teaspoon garlic powder

1 pound boneless chicken tenderloins

In a large bowl combine all ingredients except chicken and stir to mix. Add chicken and stir to coat. Cover and refrigerate for several hours or overnight.

Preheat oven to 350°F. Place chicken and marinade in baking dish. Bake for 30 minutes, basting occasionally with marinade.

Remove from oven. Baste chicken with remaining marinade and serve.

Serves Four

Per Serving

Calories 180

Carbohydrate 3 grams

Protein 23 grams

Fat 2.5 grams (1 saturated)

Fiber 0 grams

Sodium 1,060 milligrams

Diabetic exchange = 4 Very Lean Meat
WW point comparison = 3 points

This delicious Sweet and Sour Chicken is indistinguishable from one served at Chinese restaurants.

Sweet and Sour Chicken

1   pound boneless, skinless chicken breast, cut into bite-size pieces
2   teaspoons cornstarch
1   tablespoon sherry
½   teaspoon salt
½   teaspoon grated ginger (optional)

SAUCE:
½   cup peeled carrots, cut in ¼ inch slices
½   cup green pepper, cut in 1-inch pieces
½   cup pineapple chunks, well drained
½   cup Splenda Granular
¼   cup ketchup
1   tablespoon light soy sauce
⅓   cup cider vinegar
2   tablespoons cornstarch
    + 1/4 cup water

In medium bowl combine chicken, cornstarch, sherry, salt, and ginger. Toss to coat meat and set aside.

Put carrots in small saucepan with ½ cup water. Bring to boil. Boil for 1 minute. Add green pepper and boil for 1 more minute. Drain vegetables and rinse thoroughly in cold water. Add pineapple and set mixture aside.

In a small saucepan, combine Splenda, ketchup, soy sauce, and vinegar. Bring to low simmer, add cornstarch mixture, and cook, stirring, until thickened and clear. Stir in vegetables.

Heat wok until hot. Add oil. When oil is very hot, add chicken. (It should sizzle as it hits wok.) Stir-fry for 2–3 minutes until no longer pink. Remove from wok.

Combine sweet and sour sauce with chicken. Serve over brown or white rice if desired.

Serves Four

Per Serving

Calories 210	Fat 5 grams (1 saturated)
Carbohydrate 17 grams	Fiber 1 grams
Protein 24 grams	Sodium 370 milligrams

Diabetic exchange = 4 Very Lean Meat, 1 Carbohydrate
WW point comparison = 4 points

I love this sweet and spicy dish. The leftovers are great too, whether served hot or cold.

Simple Southwest Salmon

4	5-ounce salmon fillets
2	tablespoons pineapple juice
1	tablespoon lime or lemon juice
3	tablespoons Splenda Granular
2	teaspoons chili powder
¾	teaspoon ground cumin
¼	teaspoon salt
⅛	teaspoon cinnamon

Place salmon in shallow dish. Pour pineapple and lemon juice over salmon, cover, and place in refrigerator for 30 minutes.

Preheat oven to 400°F. In a small bowl combine remaining ingredients. Remove salmon from marinade. Pat spice mixture onto fillets. Place fillets on baking pan and cook for 15–20 minutes or until fish flakes easily when tested with a fork. Serve hot or, alternatively, room temperature, or cold.

Serves Four

Per Serving

Calories 225   Fat 12 grams (1.5 saturated)
Carbohydrate 2 grams Fiber 0 grams
Protein 28 grams   Sodium 220 milligrams

Diabetic exchange = 4 Lean Meat
WW point comparison = 5 points

Cookies and
Creamy Favorites

This rich vanilla pudding is great on its own or used in a parfait. To use as a pie filling, add one additional tablespoon of cornstarch.

Vanilla Pudding

3   Tbs cornstarch
⅔   cup Splenda Granular
½   cup non-fat half-and-half*
1   large egg + 1 egg yolk, slightly beaten
1¾   cups 1% milk
1½   tsp vanilla

In a medium saucepan, combine the cornstarch, Splenda, non-fat half-and-half and beaten egg. Whisk until smooth. Whisk in 1% milk. Cook and stir over medium heat until the pudding is thick and bubbly. Cook for 1 minute more. Remove from heat. Stir in the vanilla. Pour into medium bowl or divide among 5 dessert dishes. Cover with plastic wrap. Chill. Refrigerate until served.

Variation: To use as a filling for vanilla cream pie, add 1 additional tablespoon of cornstarch.

Five servings

Per serving:

Calories 110   Fat 3 grams (saturated 1)

Carbohydrate 15 grams   Fiber 0 grams

Protein 4 grams   Sodium 60 milligrams

Diabetic exchange = ½ low-fat milk, ½ carbohydrate

WW point comparison = 2 points

*Non-fat half-and-half adds richness without fat to this pudding; you may substitute evaporated skim milk or additional 1% milk for non-fat half-and-half.

This custard is a very nutritious treat. Straining the milk mixture and baking in a water bath are essential for proper texture.

Traditional Egg Custard

2   large eggs
2   large egg whites
⅔   cup Splenda Granular
2   teaspoons vanilla
2   cups 1% milk
1   cup evaporated low-fat or skim milk
    Freshly grated or ground nutmeg

Preheat oven to 325°F. In a medium bowl whisk together eggs, egg whites, Splenda, and vanilla. Set aside.

In a small saucepan bring milks to a low simmer. Whisk a small amount of hot milk into egg mixture to temper eggs. Whisk in remaining milk. Strain mixture into a large measuring cup with pouring lip or bowl.

Pour or ladle mixture into six 6-ounce custard cups or ramekins. Sprinkle with nutmeg. Place cups in large baking dish and place in oven. Pour very hot water into baking dish until it reaches halfway up the sides of the custard cups. Bake custards 50–60 minutes or until edges are set and center jiggles slightly when shaken.

Serves Six (½ cup)

Per Serving
Calories 110   Fat 3.5 grams (2 saturated)
Carbohydrate 11 grams   Fiber 1 gram
Protein 9 grams   Sodium 125 milligrams

Diabetic exchange = 1 Low-fat Milk
WW point comparison = 2 points

Cool, creamy and sweet this marvel-ous 100-calorie mousse is high in protein, vitamin C and calcium.

"Marvel-ous" Lemon Mousse

1	envelope unflavored gelatin
⅔	cup lemon juice
¾	cup Splenda Granular
	finely grated zest of 1 lemon
2	drops yellow food coloring (optional)
½	cup cottage cheese
8	ounces non-fat plain yogurt
1	egg white, pasteurized
1	Tbs sugar
¾	cup light whipped topping

Place the gelatin in a small saucepan. Add ⅓ cup of the lemon juice and let stand for 3 minutes. Place on low heat and add remaining ⅓ cup of lemon juice, Splenda, zest and food coloring if desired. Heat for 3 to 4 minutes until gelatin is completely dissolved. Transfer mixture to a bowl. Set aside and allow to cool slightly. Stir occasionally so mixture does not gel.

Purée cottage cheese and yogurt until completely smooth. Whisk purée into the lemon-gelatin mixture. Place mixture in the refrigerator to cool, whisking occasionally to prevent lumps.

In a small bowl, beat the egg white to soft peaks. Add a tablespoon of sugar and beat until stiff, but not dry. Fold into the cooled lemon mixture. Fold in light whipped topping and pour mousse into either a pretty serving bowl or individual glasses or souffle cups. Refrigerate.

Six servings

Per serving:

Calories 100

Carbohydrate 13 grams

Protein 9 grams

Fat 1.5 grams (saturated 1)

Fiber 0 grams (sugar 8)

Sodium 55 milligrams

Diabetic exchange = 1 very low-fat milk

WW point comparison = 2 points

A refreshing hot-weather treat. After freezing, soften by placing in the refrigerator.

Strawberry Frozen Yogurt

I   quart fresh strawberries, stemmed, washed, and halved
I   tablespoon lemon juice
¾   cup Splenda Granular
I   cup low-fat plain yogurt
¾   cup 1% milk

Place berries on a cookie sheet and partially freeze (15–30 minutes). Remove from freezer and coarsely puree berries with lemon juice.

In a large bowl combine Splenda, yogurt, low-fat milk, and berries.

Pour yogurt into ice-cream maker and freeze according to manufacturer's directions. Serve immediately or place into container and freeze.

Before serving, place yogurt in refrigerator for 30 minutes to soften.

Serves Six (½ cup)

Per Serving

Calories 70   Fat 1 gram (0.5 saturated)
Carbohydrate 11 grams   Fiber 2 grams
Protein 3 grams   Sodium 45 milligrams

Diabetic exchange = ½ Non-fat Milk, ½ Fruit
WW point comparison = 1 point

These kid friendly cookies are a healthy alternative to junk food.

Peanut Butter Cookies

1½	cups all-purpose flour
¾	cup Splenda Granular
1	tsp baking soda
3	Tbs brown sugar
½	tsp baking powder
1	large egg
½	cup + 2 Tbs peanut butter
2	Tbs 1% milk
¼	cup margarine
2	tsp vanilla
2	Tbs non-fat cream cheese

Preheat oven to 375 degrees. Spray cookie sheet with nonstick cooking spray.

Combine flour, baking soda, and baking powder together in a bowl. Set aside.

In a medium mixing bowl, with an electric mixer, beat peanut butter, margarine, cream cheese, Splenda, and brown sugar until creamy. Add egg, milk, and vanilla. Beat well. Stir in flour mixture.

Roll dough, by level tablespoon, into balls. Place onto cookie sheet and flatten with a fork forming a criss-cross on top of each cookie. Bake for 9 to 10 minutes. Remove from pan and cool on rack.

Twenty-six servings

Per serving:

Calories 90   Fat 5 grams (saturated 1)

Carbohydrate 8.5 grams   Fiber 0.5 grams
 (sugar 3)

Protein 3 grams   Sodium 45 milligrams

Diabetic exchange = ½ carbohydrate, 1 fat
WW point comparison = 2 points

These are soft and oh-so-full of chocolate.

Chocolate Chocolate Chip Cookies

1	cup all-purpose flour
½	cup Splenda Granular
3	Tbs Dutch-process cocoa powder (like Hershey's European)
3	Tbs brown sugar
1	egg
½	tsp baking soda
1	tsp vanilla
⅓	cup 70% vegetable oil margarine
2	Tbs 1% milk
2	Tbs prune purée
⅓	cup mini chocolate chips

Preheat oven to 375 degrees. Spray cookie sheet with nonstick cooking spray.

Combine flour, cocoa, and baking soda together in a small bowl. Set aside.

In a medium mixing bowl, with an electric mixer, beat margarine; prune purée, Splenda, and brown sugar until creamy. Add egg and vanilla. Beat well. Stir in the flour mixture, alternating with milk. Stir in chocolate chips.

Drop dough, by level tablespoons, onto cookie sheet. Press down on dough with the bottom of a slightly wet glass to flatten. Bake cookies for 8 to 10 minutes. Remove from pan and cool on rack.

Twenty-four servings

Per serving

Calories 60	Fat 3 grams (saturated 1)
Carbohydrate 8 grams (sugar 3)	Fiber 0.5 grams
Protein 1 gram	Sodium 30 milligrams

Diabetic exchange = ½ carbohydrate, ½ fat
WW point comparison = 1 point

The finishing touch to these sweet, moist, and delicious cake-like bars is the rich-tasting cream cheese frosting.

Frosted Pumpkin Bars

COOKIE BARS:

2	cups all-purpose flour
1	tsp baking powder
½	tsp baking soda
1½	tsp cinnamon
½	tsp nutmeg
¼	tsp mace
6	Tbs margarine, softened
1	2½ oz jar baby food prunes
1	15 ounce canned pumpkin purée
⅔	cup Splenda Granular
2	Tbs molasses
1½	tsp vanilla
1	egg
¼	cup raisins, finely chopped

FROSTING:

4	oz. light tub cream cheese
6	oz. non-fat cream cheese
¼	cup Splenda Granular
2	Tbs orange juice

Preheat oven to 350 degrees. Spray a 9 × 13-inch pan with nonstick baking spray.

Mix together flour, baking powder, baking soda, and spices.

In a large bowl, with an electric mixer, cream the margarine and prunes together. Add pumpkin purée, Splenda, molasses, vanilla, and egg. Beat well. Stir in flour mixture. Stir in raisins. Spoon into prepared pan and smooth. Bake for 20 minutes, or until cake springs back when lightly touched in the center. Cool on rack.

In a small bowl, with an electric mixer, beat all frosting ingredients until smooth and fluffy. Spread frosting onto cool bars. Refrigerate. Twenty-four servings.

Per serving:

Calories 75	Fat 3.5 grams (saturated 1)
Carbohydrate 8 grams	Fiber 0.5 grams
Protein 3 grams	Sodium 120 milligrams

Diabetic exchange = ½ carbohydrate, 1 fat
WW point comparison = 2 points

Pies and Crisps

The perfect ending to a heavy holiday meal.

Pumpkin Pie

1   9-inch Crust
1   large egg white beaten with 2 tsp water

FILLING

1   large egg
2   egg whites
1   15-oz can pumpkin purée (not pie filling)
½   tsp cinnamon
½   tsp ginger
¼   tsp allspice (optional)
¾   cup Splenda Granular
¼   tsp ground cloves
1   tsp vanilla
1   Tbs molasses
2   tsp cornstarch
1   12-oz can evaporated skim milk

Preheat oven to 425 degrees. Place pie shell in lower ⅓ of oven and bake for 15 minutes, pressing down on any air bubbles that form. Remove from oven and brush with beaten egg white and water mixture. Set aside to dry.

In a large bowl, whisk 1 large egg and egg whites. Add pumpkin, Splenda, molasses, cornstarch, spices, and vanilla. Mix well. Stir in milk.

Pour the filling into pre-baked crust. Bake at 425 degrees for 10 minutes, then reduce the heat to 350 degrees and bake 30 to 35 minutes longer, or until a knife inserted near the center comes out clean. Cool pie on wire rack.

Eight servings

Per serving:

Calories 200

Carbohydrate 26

Protein 8 grams

Fat 7 grams (saturated 1.5)

Fiber 3 grams

Sodium 160 milligrams

Diabetic exchange = 1 carbohydrate, 1 fat, ½ low-fat milk, ½ vegetable

WW point comparison = 4 points

Luscious, and yet so light. This creamy no-bake pie is a nice change from traditional lemon meringue.

Lemon Chiffon Pie

1	Graham Cracker Crust recipe, baked, page 78
⅓	cup water
1	envelope (2½ tsp) unflavored gelatin
1	large egg + 2 large egg yolks, beaten (reserve whites to use below)
¾	cup Splenda Granular
½	cup lemon juice
2	tsp grated lemon rind
4	large pasteurized egg whites (or 2 regular egg whites)
¼	tsp cream of tartar
3	Tbs Splenda Granular
1	cup light whipped topping, thawed

Place water in a small heavy saucepan and sprinkle gelatin on top. Let set for 3 minutes to soften gelatin. Whisk in beaten eggs, Splenda, lemon juice, and lemon rind. Stirring constantly with a wooden spoon or heatproof rubber spatula, heat over medium heat until the mixture thickens enough to coat spoon or spatula. Pour the mixture into a large bowl and refrigerate for 45 minutes to 1 hour until mixture mounds when dropped from a spoon, but is not set.

In a large bowl, beat egg whites and cream of tartar until foamy. Continue to beat; gradually add Splenda and beat until stiff but not dry. Using a large rubber spatula or spoon, gently fold egg whites into cooled lemon mixture. Fold in whipped topping.

Spoon filling into crust and refrigerate for at least 3 hours.

Eight servings

Per serving:

Calories 140
Carbohydrate 18 grams
Protein 6 grams

Fat 6 grams (saturated 2)
Fiber 0 grams
Sodium 145 milligrams

Diabetic exchange = 1 carbohydrate, 1 medium fat meat
WW point comparison = 3 points

An old-fashioned, homestyle apple pie made with a sensational streusel topping.

Sour Cream Apple Pie

1   unbaked 9-inch pie crust
2   large eggs
1   cup light sour cream
¾   cup Splenda Granular
2   tablespoons all-purpose flour
2   teaspoons vanilla
¼   teaspoon salt
2½ cups peeled, thinly sliced, baking apples

STREUSEL TOPPING:
4   tablespoons all-purpose flour
3   tablespoons butter
⅓   cup Splenda Granular
1   teaspoon cinnamon

Preheat oven to 425°F. Bake pie crust for 15 minutes. Remove from oven. Cool. Set aside.

In a large bowl, lightly beat together eggs, sour cream, Splenda Granular, flour, vanilla, and salt. Stir in apples and pour into the prebaked pie shell. Bake for 15 minutes. Reduce heat to 350°F and bake for 20 minutes more, covering edges of piecrust with foil as needed to prevent overbrowning.

While pie is baking, combine the topping ingredients. Remove pie from oven and sprinkle on topping. Return pie to oven and bake an additional 20 minutes. Cool completely before serving.

Serves Eight

Per Serving

Calories 190	Fat 11 grams (5 saturated)
Carbohydrate 20 grams	Fiber 1 gram
Protein 4 grams	Sodium 150 milligrams

Diabetic exchange = 1 Fruit, ½ Carbohydrate, 2 Fat
WW point comparison = 4 points

A winning combination of that tastes like a thin mint cookie.

Chocolate Mint Cream Pie

1 Double Chocolate Crumb Crust recipe, baked, page 74

FILLING:

¾   cup Splenda Granular
3   Tbs cornstarch
2   Tbs Dutch-process cocoa powder
½   cup non-fat half-and-half
1½ cups 1% milk
1   large egg, beaten
⅓   cup semi-sweet chocolate chips
1   tsp vanilla

TOPPING:

1½ cup light whipped topping, thawed
2   Tbs Splenda Granular
¼   tsp mint extract (scant)

In a medium saucepan, combine the Splenda, cornstarch, and cocoa powder. Stir in the milk and half-and-half; whisk until cornstarch completely dissolves. Add the beaten egg and whisk. Bring mixture to a low simmer over medium heat, stirring constantly. As the mixture starts to thicken remove from heat briefly and stir thoroughly, including corners of the pot to discourage lumps. Add chocolate, return to heat, simmer and stir for 1 to 2 minutes. Pudding should be thick and smooth. Add vanilla, stir, and remove from heat.

Pour hot filling into piecrust. Cover surface with plastic wrap. Cool completely on rack, then refrigerate until completely chilled. In a medium bowl, fold Splenda and mint extract into whipped topping. Spread over pie. Refrigerate.

Flavor variation: Chocolate Peppermint Pie—substitute peppermint extract for mint. Eight servings.

Per serving:

Calories 200	Fat 8 grams (saturated 4)
Carbohydrate 27 grams	Fiber 1 gram
Protein 5 grams	Sodium 150 milligrams

Diabetic exchange = 2 carbohydrate, 1 lean meat, 1 fat
WW point comparison = 4 points

A great-tasting deep, dark chocolate crust with a lot less fat and sugar than the store bought crusts.

Double Chocolate Crumb Crust

- 1 cup chocolate graham cracker crumbs (about 14 squares)
- 1 Tbs Dutch-process cocoa powder (like Hershey's European)
- ¼ cup Splenda Granular
- 1 Tbs margarine or butter, melted
- 1 Tbs canola oil
- 1 large egg white (about 3 Tbs)

Preheat oven to 350 degrees. Lightly coat a 9-inch pie pan with nonstick cooking spray.

Combine crumbs in a small bowl or food processor (pulse to make crumbs from crackers). Add cocoa powder, Splenda, margarine, and oil, and stir or pulse. Add egg white and stir well, or pulse again. Pour crumb mixture into pie plate. With your fingers, the back of a spoon, or with a sheet of plastic wrap, press down on the crumbs until they coat the bottom and sides of the pie plate. Bake 8 to 10 minutes.

Eight servings

Per serving:

Calories 90
Carbohydrate 12
Protein 2 grams

Fat 4.5 grams (saturated 0.5)
Fiber 0 grams
Sodium 95 milligrams

Diabetic exchange = 1 carbohydrate, 1 fat

A scrumptious dessert recipe sent to me by a fan of
my first book.

Kim's Mixed Berry Crisp

2   16-ounce bags frozen mixed berries, thawed slightly
¾   cup Splenda Granular
1½ tablespoons cornstarch

TOPPING
¾   cup old-fashioned rolled oats
¾   cup Splenda Granular
¾   teaspoon cinnamon
1   tablespoon margarine
1   egg white

Preheat oven to 350°F. Set aside 9 × 13-inch pan.

In a large bowl toss berries with Splenda and cornstarch. Pour into pan.

In a small bowl cut margarine into oats, Splenda,
and cinnamon. Gently stir in egg white and sprinkle
over berries. Bake for 30 minutes or until bubbling.

Serves Eight

Per Serving
Calories 135   Fat 2.5 grams (0 saturated)
Carbohydrate 28 grams Fiber 6 grams
Protein 2 grams   Sodium 15 milligrams

Diabetic exchange = 1 Fruit, ½ Carbohydrate, ½ Fat
WW point comparison = 2 points

Phyllo (filo) dough is found in the frozen food section. To keep unused sheets from drying out before use, cover with a damp cloth.

Apple Strudel

4	cups finely sliced, peeled apples (about 1½–1¾ pounds fresh)
⅓	cup Splenda Granular
¼	cup raisins, finely chopped
¼	cup pecans, finely chopped
1½	tsp cinnamon
1	Tbs plain bread crumbs
6	sheets phyllo dough (16½ × 12 inches)
½	Tbs butter, melted
1	Tbs powdered sugar

Preheat oven to 350 degrees. Spray a baking sheet with nonstick cooking spray.

In a large bowl, combine apples and next 5 ingredients. Set aside.

Spread a large piece of plastic wrap or wax paper onto a large surface. Carefully lay 1 piece of the phyllo dough onto the work surface, with the long side closest to you. Spray the entire sheet with cooking spray. Lay another sheet of dough on top of the first. Spray again. Repeat until all 6 sheets are stacked. Spoon the apple mixture in a long strip across the center of the dough, leaving 3 inches on all sides. Starting with the long side of the dough that is closest to you lift the empty dough up over the apples. Fold side ends and far side of dough up and over the apples to enclose. Carefully, use the paper to help you turn the strudel seam side down onto the prepared baking sheet. Brush with melted butter. Bake 40 to 45 minutes, or until the pastry is golden brown. Cool slightly and sift powdered sugar over entire strudel. Best when served warm.

Eight servings

Per serving:

Calories 160
Carbohydrate 26 grams
Protein 2 grams

Fat 6 grams (saturated 1)
Fiber 3 grams
Sodium 75 milligrams

Diabetic exchange = 1 fruit, ½ carbohydrate, 1 fat
WW point comparison = 3 points

Using egg white to help bind the crust lowers the fat in this popular graham crust.

Graham Cracker Pie Crust

1   cup graham cracker crumbs (about 16 squares)
2   Tbs Splenda Granular
1   Tbs margarine or butter, melted
1   Tbs canola oil
2   Tbs egg white

Preheat oven to 350 degrees. Lightly coat a 9-inch pie pan with nonstick cooking spray.

Combine crumbs in a small bowl or food processor (pulse to make crumbs from crackers). Add Splenda, margarine, and oil, and stir or pulse. Add egg white and stir well, or pulse again. Pour crumb mixture into pie plate. With your fingers, the back of a spoon, or with a sheet of plastic wrap, press down on the crumbs until they coat the bottom and sides of the pie plate. Bake 8 to 10 minutes. Remove and cool.

Eight servings

Per serving:

Calories 90   Fat 4.5 grams (saturated 0.5)
Carbohydrate 12 grams   Fiber 0 grams
Protein 1 gram   Sodium 105 milligrams

Diabetic exchange = 1 carbohydrate, 1 fat

Cakes and Cheesecakes

So easy, so delicious. I love this served warm with a dollop of light whipped topping.

Fresh Banana Cake

3	small bananas, mashed (about 1 cup purée)
2	Tbs canola oil
⅔	cup Splenda Granular
1	Tbs molasses
1	large egg
1	large egg white
½	cup nonfat plain yogurt
2	tsp vanilla
1½	cups cake flour
1	tsp baking powder
¾	tsp baking soda
2	tsp powdered sugar

Preheat oven to 350 degrees. Spray a 9-inch cake pan with nonstick baking spray.

Place banana purée in a large mixing bowl. Whisk in next 7 ingredients (oil through vanilla). Sift cake flour, baking powder, and baking soda into the bowl. Stir to blend in dry ingredients.

Spoon batter into prepared pan. Bake for 30 minutes or until a toothpick inserted into the center of the cake comes out clean. Cool in pan. Sift powdered sugar over cake just prior to serving if desired.

Eight servings

Per serving:

Calories 130   Fat 3.5 (saturated 0)
Carbohydrate 21 grams   Fiber 1 gram
Protein 3 grams   Sodium 300 milligrams

Diabetic exchange = 1½ carbohydrate, ½ fat
WW point comparison = 3 points

Ginger, cinnamon, and molasses combine to give this gingerbread a traditional old-fashioned flavor.

Grandma's Gingerbread

1	cup all-purpose flour
½	cup whole wheat flour
1	teaspoon ginger
1	teaspoon cinnamon
¼	teaspoon cloves
1	teaspoon baking soda
¼	cup molasses
3	tablespoons canola oil
¼	cup prune puree or
1	2.5-ounce jar baby food prunes
1	large egg
½	cup water
½	cup Splenda Granular

Preheat oven to 350°F. Coat an 8-inch square cake pan with nonstick cooking spray.

In a medium bowl sift together flours, spices, and baking soda. Set aside.

In a large mixing bowl whisk together remaining ingredients.

Fold dry ingredients into molasses mixture and then pour batter into prepared pan. Bake for 18–20 minutes or until top springs back when touched. Cool and serve with light whipped topping if desired.

Serves Nine

Per Serving

Calories 160

Carbohydrate 26 grams

Protein 3 grams

Fat 5 grams (0.5 saturated)

Fiber 2 grams

Sodium 150 milligrams

Diabetic exchange = 1½ Carbohydrate, 1 Fat

WW point comparison = 3 points

A moist and light, one-bowl chocolate cake. Dress it up with whipped topping and sliced strawberries for a fancy dessert.

Unbelievable Chocolate Cake

¼   cup canola oil

I   large egg

I   tsp vanilla

¼   cup brown sugar, packed (be sure it is fresh, with no hard lumps)

I   cup Splenda Granular

I   cup low-fat buttermilk

1¼ cups cake flour

I   tsp baking soda

I   tsp baking powder

¼   cup Dutch-process cocoa powder (like Hershey's European)

¼   cup hot water

2   tsp powdered sugar (optional)

Preheat oven to 350. Spray an 8 × 8-inch baking pan with nonstick baking spray.

In a large bowl whisk together the oil and the egg for 1 minute until the mixture is thick and frothy. Add the vanilla, brown sugar, and Splenda and beat with the whisk for 2 more minutes until the mixture is thick and smooth and the sugars have been thoroughly beaten into the mixture. Add 1 cup buttermilk and mix.

Using a sifter or a metal sieve, sift the flour, baking powder, baking soda, and cocoa powder into the liquid mixture. Whisk vigorously for 1 to 2 minutes until the batter is nice and smooth.

Pour the hot water into the batter and whisk one more time until the batter is again nice and smooth. The batter will be thin. Pour the batter into the prepared cake pan and tap the pan on the counter to level the surface and to help remove any air bubbles.

Bake for 18 to 20 minutes or just until the center springs back when touched and a cake tester or toothpick comes out clean. Do not overcook. Remove the cake from the oven and cool. Sift optional powder sugar over cake to serve.

Nine servings

Per serving:

Calories 160	Fat 7 grams (saturated 1)
Carbohydrate 22 grams	Fiber 1 grams
Protein 3 grams	Sodium 200 milligrams

Diabetic exchange = 1½ servings carbohydrate, 1 fat
WW point comparison = 3 points

This cake, pictured on the cover of my first book, was featured on the Food Network. Serve with the Strawberry Coulis on page 98

Heavenly Cheesecake

1	8- or 9-inch baked Cheesecake Crumb Crust, page 78
1	cup low-fat cottage cheese
8	oz tub-style light cream cheese
8	oz non-fat cream cheese, room temperature
1¼	cups Splenda Granular
2	Tbs all-purpose flour
2	Tbs cornstarch
1	tsp vanilla extract
½	tsp almond extract
3	large egg whites
1	large egg
1¼	cups light sour cream

Preheat oven to 350 degrees. Wrap 8-inch (or 9-inch) springform pan with crust tightly in heavy-duty foil to make waterproof.

Place cottage cheese into a food processor or blender. Purée until completely smooth. Spoon into a large mixing bowl and add nonfat and light cream cheeses. Beat on medium speed, with an electric mixer until creamy. Add the Splenda, flour, cornstarch, and extracts, and beat on low until smooth. Add large egg and then egg whites beating just briefly after each addition to incorporate. Stir in the sour cream with a large spoon. Pour into the prepared crust and smooth top. Place the foil-wrapped pan in a large, deep baking pan and pour boiling water into pan until it reaches halfway up the outside of the cheesecake pan.

Bake for 60 minutes or until sides of cake appear firm and center jiggles slightly. (For a 9-inch pan, bake 50 to 55 minutes.) Turn off heat, open oven door, and let cheesecake cool in the oven for 30 minutes. Remove from water bath and finish cooling. Refrigerate at least 6 hours before serving.

Twelve servings

Per serving:

Calories 180	Fat 8 grams (saturated 5)
Carbohydrate 15 grams	Fiber 0 grams
Protein 11 grams	Sodium 350milligrams

Diabetic exchange = 1 carbohydrate, 1½ lean meat
WW point comparison = 4 points

If you like Key Lime pie, you'll love this light, no-bake cheesecake.

Key Lime Cheesecake

1	9-inch Cheesecake Crumb Crust (page 78)
1	envelope of unflavored gelatin (2½ tsp)
¾	cup key lime juice (fresh or bottled)
2	large eggs, lightly beaten
1	cup Splenda Granular
8	oz tub-style light cream cheese
8	oz non-fat cream cheese, room temperature
4	large pasteurized egg whites (or 2 regular egg whites)
¾	cup Splenda Granular
1½	cups light whipped topping

In a medium saucepan, dissolve the gelatin in the key lime juice for three minutes. Add 1 cup of Splenda, and the 2 beaten eggs. Whisk until smooth.

Place on stove, turn heat to medium while stirring, and cook for 10 minutes or until mixture thickens. Remove from heat. Cool slightly.

Place the cream cheese in a large bowl and beat on medium speed with an electric mixer until creamy. Slowly add the lime mixture and beat on low until smooth. Refrigerate mixture until thoroughly cooled, stirring every 10 minutes.

In a separate bowl, beat the egg whites until foamy or until soft peaks begin form (this can take

5 minutes or more with pasteurized egg whites). Slowly add the ¾ cup Splenda until incorporated. Fold egg-white mixture into the chilled lime-cheese mix.

Pour onto prepared crust. Refrigerate until set, about 2 hours. Spread whipped topping over cake.

Twelve servings

Per serving:

Calories 160	Fat 7.5 grams (saturated 4)
Carbohydrate 16 grams	Fiber 0 grams
Protein 7 grams	Sodium 270 milligrams

Diabetic exchange = 1 carbohydrate, 1 lean meat, 1 fat
WW point comparison = 4 points

What could be better than chocolate, cherries and cheesecake in a beautiful parfait presentation.

Black Forest Cheesecake Parfaits

1½ cups frozen black cherries, thawed

2 tablespoons Splenda Granular

½ teaspoon almond extract

½ cup chocolate graham-cracker crumbs

2 tablespoons Splenda Granular

1½ tablespoons cocoa powder

½ tablespoon butter, melted

4 ounces light tub-style cream cheese, room temperature

4 ounces fat-free cream cheese, room temperature

½ cup light sour cream

¼ cup Splenda Granular

1½ cups light whipped topping

Select 6 tall stemmed glasses (an 8-ounce wineglass or champagne glass is ideal). In a small bowl mix cherries, 2 tablespoons Splenda, and almond extract. Set aside.

In another small bowl mix graham-cracker crumbs, 2 tablespoons Splenda, cocoa powder, and butter. Set aside.

In a medium mixing bowl beat cream cheeses with an electric mixer until creamy. Add sour cream and

Splenda and beat until smooth. Fold in whipped topping with a spoon or spatula. In the bottom of each glass, place 1 tablespoon graham-cracker mix. Press down with spoon. Place about 3 tablespoons of cream cheese mix on top of each. (You will use only half of the cheese mixture for the 6 glasses.) Divide the cherries among the glasses, placing them on top of the cream cheese layer. Add one more layer of cream cheese. Finish the parfait by topping each with 1 tablespoon of crumbs.

These can be enjoyed immediately, or place them in the refrigerator until you are ready to serve them.

Serves Six

Per Serving

Calories 200	Fat 8 grams (2 saturated)
Carbohydrate 24 grams	Fiber 1 gram
Protein 7 grams	Sodium 290 milligrams

Diabetic exchange = 1½ Carbohydrate, 1 Lean Meat, 1 Fat
WW point comparison = 4 points

Condiments, Dressings, and Sauces

Dip chicken, ribs, or any other food you wish into this versatile sauce.

Quick Smooth Barbecue Dipping Sauce

1   8-ounce can tomato sauce
2   tablespoons water
1   tablespoon Worcestershire sauce
1   tablespoon cider vinegar
4   tablespoons Splenda Granular
1   teaspoon honey
    Pinch onion powder
    Pinch salt

Place all ingredients in a small saucepan, stir, and cook for 5 minutes over low heat. (For a thicker sauce cook additional 5 minutes.)

Serves Six (2 tablespoons)

Per Serving

Calories 15   Fat 0 grams (0 saturated)
Carbohydrate 4 grams   Fiber .5 grams
Protein 0.5 grams   Sodium 210 milligrams

Diabetic exchange = free exchange
WW point comparison = 0 points

Spread this on cold turkey sandwiches or plain crackers, serve it with roast pork, or add a drop or two of red food coloring and jar it up as a lovely gift.

Cranberry Chutney

I	teaspoon canola oil
I	large shallot, finely chopped (⅓ cup)
I	12-ounce package cranberries
½	cup Splenda Granular
½	cup orange juice
⅓	cup cider vinegar
I	tablespoon brown sugar
½	teaspoon ground ginger
	Scant ¼ teaspoon red pepper flakes
I	tablespoon orange zest

In a large saucepan heat oil and sauté shallot 3–4 minutes or until softened. Add all remaining ingredients except zest and bring to a boil. Lower heat and simmer for 15 minutes, stirring occasionally. Add zest and cook 15 more minutes or until thickened. Cool and store in refrigerator. Serve cool or room temperature.

Serves Twelve (2 tablespoons)

Per serving

Calories 35	Fat 0 grams (0 saturated)
Carbohydrate 8 grams	Fiber I gram
Protein 0 grams	Sodium 0 milligrams

Diabetic exchange = ½ Fruit
WW point comparison = I point

This dressing pairs especially well with salads containing fruit or nuts like baby greens with strawberries or red leaf lettuce with pear slices and pecans.

Sweet Balsamic Vinaigrette

3   tablespoons red wine vinegar
2   tablespoons balsamic vinegar
2   tablespoons orange juice
2   tablespoons Splenda Granular (or 3 Splenda packets)
1   clove garlic, minced
3   tablespoons extra virgin olive oil
2   teaspoons Dijon mustard
     Fresh ground pepper

Whisk first 5 ingredients together in a small bowl. Whisk in olive oil one tablespoon at a time to thoroughly incorporate. Whisk in mustard. Add pepper to taste.

Serves Six (about 2 tablespoons)

Per Serving
Calories 70   Fat 7 grams (1 saturated)
Carbohydrate 2 grams   Fiber 0 grams
Protein 0 grams   Sodium 0 milligrams

Diabetic exchange = 1½ Fat
WW point comparison = 2 points

This is a copy-cat of the popular bottled dressing without the fat or sugar. You must taste it to believe it!

Fat-Free Catalina (Sweet French) Dressing

1	cup cold water
⅓	cup Splenda Granular
3	tablespoons tomato paste
1½	teaspoons cornstarch
½	teaspoon salt
⅛	teaspoon garlic powder
⅛	teaspoon chili powder (optional)

Place all the ingredients in a small saucepan and whisk until the cornstarch is completely dissolved. Place over low heat and cook until dressing comes to a boil and thickens and clears. Remove from heat and cool. Cover and refrigerate.

Serves Eight (2 tablespoons)

Per Serving

Calories 10	Fat 0 grams (0 saturated)
Carbohydrate 3 grams	Fiber 0 grams
Protein 0 grams	Sodium 180 milligrams

Diabetic exchange = 1 Fat
WW point comparison = 1 point

Use this unstrained as a chunky sauce for ice cream or plain cakes, or strained as a coulis, drizzled onto plates or elegant desserts.

Strawberry Sauce and Coulis

2	cups strawberries, fresh or frozen
⅓	cup Splenda Granular
1	Tbs lemon juice
½	cup water
2	tsp cornstarch
1	Tbs orange liqueur (optional)

Place the berries in a heavy, non-aluminum saucepan. Add remaining ingredients (except liqueur) and stir until cornstarch dissolves. Place over medium heat and bring to a boil. Turn down and simmer for 1 minute, stirring constantly. Remove from heat and stir in liqueur if desired.

Variation: For smooth Strawberry Coulis, strain the strawberry sauce through a fine strainer or sieve, pressing on the fruit to drain all the liquid. Throw away pulp.

Eight servings (2 tablespoons each)

Per serving:

Calories 15	Fat 0 grams (saturated 0)
Carbohydrate 3 grams (sugar 1)	Fiber 0 grams
Protein 0 grams	Sodium 0 grams
Diabetic exchange = 1 free food	
WW point comparison = 0 points	

You are certain to find many uses for this delicious, oh-so-chocolatey sauce.

Dark Chocolate Sauce

¼ cup Dutch-processed cocoa powder,

⅓ cup Splenda Granular

¼ cup water

⅓ cup fat-free half-and-half

1 tablespoon light corn syrup

1 ounce semisweet chocolate, chopped

1 teaspoon vanilla

Combine cocoa, Splenda, water, half-and-half, and corn syrup in a small saucepan. Whisk over low heat until mixture is smooth and hot. (Do not boil.)

Remove from heat and whisk in chocolate and vanilla until chocolate melts and sauce is smooth again.

Serves Eight (2 tablespoons)

Per Serving

Calories 45   Fat 2 grams (1 saturated)

Carbohydrate 8 grams   Fiber 1 gram

Protein 1 gram   Sodium 15 milligrams

Diabetic exchange = ½ Carbohydrate

WW point comparison = 1 point

Notes

Marlene Koch is a registered dietitian who specializes in good food and good health. Combining her love for great-tasting food with her knowledge of nutrition, she has taught for the American Culinary Association (the national association of professional chefs), is a popular instructor at professional cooking schools, and is a frequent guest on network television and radio programs. Her recipes have been featured on The Food Network and *The Today Show* as well as in magazines such as *Cooking Light, Diabetic Cooking,* and *Low Carb Energy.*

For more information on cooking and Splenda or Marlene's publications, visit her on the Web at www.marlenekoch.com.

available at booksellers nationwide